Sidney George Fisher

The Laws of Race

As Connected With Slavery

Sidney George Fisher

The Laws of Race
As Connected With Slavery

ISBN/EAN: 9783744732772

Printed in Europe, USA, Canada, Australia, Japan

Cover: Foto ©ninafisch / pixelio.de

More available books at **www.hansebooks.com**

THE LAWS OF RACE,

AS CONNECTED WITH

𝔖𝔩𝔞𝔟𝔢𝔯𝔶.

BY THE AUTHOR OF "THE LAW OF THE TERRITORIES," "RUSTIC RHYMES," ETC.

"Seal up the mouth of outrage for awhile,
Till we can clear these ambiguities,
And show their spring, their head, their true descent."

ROMEO AND JULIET.

PHILADELPHIA:

WILLIS P. HAZARD, 724 CHESTNUT STREET.

1860.

Contents.

RACE.

"Black spirits and white,
Red spirits and gray:
Mingle, mingle, mingle,
You that mingle may."
MACBETH.

THE attention of government, the debates of Congress, the public press, and the thoughts of the people, have been almost exclusively occupied, for the last five or six years, by questions of law and policy, arising out of the all-absorbing topic of slavery. To understand that subject, however, we must go deeper. Slavery does not rest on the Constitution or laws as a basis, but they on it. It is not the creature, but the director of our policy. It is a permanent, commanding fact in our country, and may not be disregarded. To manage it rightly, is the great problem of our politics, for it has power over us and our destiny. Slavery has a nature of its own, according to which we must shape our measures, if we would be safe and prosper.

What is that nature? The subject is usually discussed as if the question involved was slavery in the abstract; and much is said about its injustice, its cruelty, its inexpediency. The obvious truth, that slavery implies a slave and a master, seems to be generally overlooked. Here the negro is the slave, and the white man the master, each of them strongly marked and contrasted, in their mental, moral, and physical qualities. These qualities must control the character of any relations between the parties. To understand slavery, therefore, we must study the nature of the white man and of the negro. Out of the principles of their respective organizations, we may be sure, slavery has grown and by them will be controlled, do what we may. Those principles were impressed upon each by Divine will, and the consequences that flow from them have the same source. As in the tumult of the ocean, in the countless variety of vegetable and animal life covering the earth, unity displays itself in diversity, and law reigns amid apparent confusion, so in the rush and strife and complexity of human affairs, the truth that was from the beginning, presides over and directs the storm. This controlling truth, this *causa causans,* if we can find it out, will afford a clue to guide us through the labyrinth of what is called the slavery question, and direct our efforts to definite and attainable ends. Obedience to its behests is the only path of safety.

The researches of ingenious men, during the present age, have produced results which are gradually leading the educated mind of Europe and this country to the conclusion, that most of the difficult and complicated social and political questions which agitate the world, if not all of them, resolve themselves into the question of race. The science of ethnology is yet in its infancy. Much ground is unexplored, and some hypotheses wait for inductive demonstration. The origin of man and of species, the definite classification of the branches of the human family, the laws by which they mingle or refuse to mingle, and other questions, remain open for investigation and discovery.

But some progress has been made. The strata of the earth have been examined, the anatomy and physical structure of races of men and animals, have been studied and compared, the antique monuments of pre-historic eras, the earliest written records, the religions and the laws, the languages, literature and art, the manners and customs of nations, have been investigated, and all these inquiries, intellectual, moral and physical, have resulted in the discovery of certain truths of great practical importance; of commanding importance, indeed, to us, as a nation. Those ethnical principles which concern the present topic, and seem now established as scientific truths, may be thus stated.

Men are divided into certain distinct races, or species, and these again into sub-species or permanent varieties, also distinct. These species refuse to amalgamate, the hybrids being more or less unprolific with each other, and exhibiting a constant tendency to return to the pure race; so that the separation of the races is preserved, and the creation of a new race impossible.

These races are distinguished by clearly defined and different organic physical structure, and also by different mental and moral traits, more especially by inequality of mental and moral force, and have been so distinguished, without change, in all ages.

These races have originated, or been distributed, in certain zones of climate favorable to their nature, and do not thrive, and flourish, and maintain themselves, in other portions of the earth.*

Of these races, the white is the highest in the scale, the black the lowest. The average size of the brain of the white, is 92 cubic inches, of the negro 83, of the Hottentot and Australian 75.† The white alone possesses the intellectual and moral energy which creates that development of free

---

* Gobineau, sur l'inegalité des Races humain. The Races of Men, by Robert Knox. Types of Mankind, by Nott and Gliddon.

† Types of Mankind, by Nott and Gliddon, p. 454.

government, industry, science, literature, and the arts, which we call civilization. The black can neither originate, maintain, nor comprehend civilization. He is by nature a barbarian. When in contact with the white race, he naturally and willingly yields to it, and becomes its servant. The two races have exhibited these characteristics in all ages.

Various causes have brought together in this country, all the races ; the white, the yellow, and the black ; Teutonic, Celt, Mongol, and Negro. The qualities of each, are so many forces which are to act upon our destiny, according to their own respective laws of being. As the present discussion relates only to the subject of slavery, if the conclusions of ethnical science above stated be correct, these three consequences logically follow :

The white race must of necessity, by reason of its superiority, govern the negro, wherever the two live together.

The two races can never amalgamate, and form a new species of man, but must remain forever distinct; though mulattoes and other grades always exist, because constantly renewed.

Each race has a tendency to occupy exclusively that portion of the country suited to its nature.

These truths, if they be truths, are worth attention. They *must* rule our politics and our destiny, either by the constitution or over it, either with the

Union or without it, and no wit or force of man is strong enough to resist them. They are the higher law, to which we must submit on pain of destruction, just as we must submit to the laws of steam and electricity, of winds and waves, of earth and iron, of acid and alkali ; and as Lord Bacon says, by submitting, govern, and direct them to our advantage.

It is therefore a matter of serious interest, to discover how far our constitution or laws, and the governing public opinion of the people, agree with this higher law,—these controlling principles and qualities of race, which form the plan of human organization. The object of this essay is to show that they do agree.

It is not surprising, that what is called the slavery question, but which ought to be called the negro question, absorbs so largely the attention of our people, for in it are involved, not merely their temporal interests, but all those questions of religion and morals, which in every age, have most deeply stirred the thoughts, and touched the feelings of men. Slavery is apparently a violent contradiction of our position and pretensions as a free and Christian people. We proclaim liberty, in our constitution and our laws, as the foundation-principle of our government, yet we deny to four millions of men, under our control, all civil rights whatever. The constitution was not made for them we say, they are not part of our people, they are not even men, they are property. We are professors of Christianity, we have schools, we have churches, we have the bible, we have the benign scheme of Christian morality, which teaches the law of love as the rule of conduct, and which sanctifies the domestic relations, the fountain source of social happiness. Nevertheless our schools, our churches, the bible and the sacredness of home, its ties and its joys, are for ourselves, and not for the negro. We darken his mind with ignorance, we make him an instrument of gain, a beast of burden, and deliver him up without protection, to the callousness of cupidity, the recklessness of passion, the brutality of lust. We do this with forethought and design, we do it by law; we, who are not Austrians, Russians, or Turks, but Saxon men, transplanted Englishmen, who have brought with us *magna charta* and the common law, who are republicans and democrats, and who assert, with sincerity and truth too, our love of freedom and our reverence for human rights!

Surely this is a strange anomaly. The world has a right to ask us, we ought to ask ourselves, why do we this thing? The answer is, because we cannot do otherwise. We have brought the negro to our shores, and therefore slavery with him. He

2

cannot participate in our liberty, our constitution, our churches, and our schools. We cannot, if we would, make him a partner in our civilization. Slavery is the necessary result of his nature and of our nature.

The difference and natural inequality of the two races, white and black, therefore govern what is called the slavery question, and all the constitutional and sectional questions dependent on it. The negro is the inferior,—born for subordination and servitude, which has been his lot in all ages, when brought within the sphere of the white race. The Saxon, the highest type of the white race, will not live with the negro on terms of equality,—on any other terms than those of marked and recognized inequality. This is the relation between them wherever they do live together. What position of inequality the negro shall hold, is for the Saxon to determine, and his judgment must be guided by his interest, his safety, his pride, and also by his sense of justice and benevolence. But he must be the judge, he who lives with the negro, not another who does not. The Saxon man in the South lives alongside of the negro. The latter is so strong in numbers, that he is a dangerous companion, unless his obedience and subjection can be rendered certain. The negro is the laborer, and his labor is the basis on which is erected the whole fabric of the wealth and prosperity of the Saxon. The negro is by nature indolent and improvident. The motives which stimulate other races to industry, have weak influence over him. Without some system of compulsion he will not work. He is also ignorant; the animal predominates in his character over the intellectual and moral, his mind is weak, his passions are strong, he therefore requires restraint and guidance, both for his own good, and that of the superior race, for otherwise he would sink into helpless, hopeless vice, idleness, and misery. The Saxon, to whose control the negro has been committed, has determined that slavery is the plan of government which suits him better than any other. It furnishes a system of police, watchfulness, and restraint which secures obedience, industry, order, and temperance on the part of the negro, by which the safety and prosperity of the white race are maintained and promoted; it secures also, the physical well-being of the negro, by giving to his master an interest in that well-being. The labor of the slave is the source of wealth; labor comes of health and strength; health and strength of sufficient food, raiment, shelter, and regular, but not excessive, work. The Saxon residing in the South with the negro, has chosen this system for his government. He claims the right to choose it or any other, and he claims this right by prerogative of race, by the decree of nature, which made him superior to the negro, in force of mind and character, and therefore his ruler. He will not relinquish this claim. He cannot if he would. His right to it runs in his veins, beats in his breast, and is founded on immemorial usage, from the earliest periods of recorded history. He will resist whilst he can, any power that shall attempt to interfere with that right, or dictate to him how he shall use it.

On the other hand, this same Saxon or Teutonic man, is a lover of liberty. His is the only race that does love it, and has been able to acquire and keep it. He loves instinctively, personal liberty, power over himself, freedom from the will of another. He loves also political liberty; that is to say, a share of political power, so that he may consent to any control to which he does submit, and form himself a part of the government he obeys. To such a man, slavery in the abstract is revolting; but his love of liberty is, in part, love of power. He sympathizes, therefore, with the oppressed, provided he be not the oppressor, and would gladly break all chains of bondage, except those which he imposes. These characteristics of the Saxon, his practical ability and faculty for abstract thought; his passion for conquest and power, and his love of liberty, truth, and justice, whilst they make him a colonizer and a ruler, also render his rule beneficent. Churches, charities, law, order, industry, wealth, arts, and letters, follow his footsteps. He is not a destroyer, but a builder; and although he will be a master where he can, he is a kind master, and his authority is a shelter and a protection.

Out of these relative qualities of the negro and the Tuetonic races, and more especially of the Saxon, the highest type of the latter, grows the apparently anomalous fact that slavery exists in this country; that it is sanctioned and protected by the laws and the constitution, and by public opinion. These qualities also explain the difference of sentiment between North and South on the subject of slavery. The Saxon loves power; his is the conquering, colonizing race. Wherever he goes,—to India, to China, to Australia, or America,—he subdues and governs the weaker and lower races. In the South, he is in contact with the negro, the weakest and lowest of all. He must therefore control the negro. In the North, the aborigines having withered and vanished before him, because they would neither submit to him nor be civilized by him, the Saxon finds no race inferior to his own, or so inferior, that he can assume any marked and positive dominion over it, or so numerous as to require any laws to insure

2*

his superiority. Now, at least, Saxon, Celt, and German, live together harmoniously, though, perhaps, this is only because as yet the Saxon practically predominates and governs. But a question has arisen between the Saxon of the North and the negro of the South, as to which shall possess and cultivate vast regions of unoccupied fertile land, the property of the whole white race of this country, represented by its government. True to his instincts of conqueror, colonizer, founder, the Saxon of the North claims this land for himself; he claims that he, and not the negro, shall occupy and till it, live on it and by it. Moved by the same inherent spirit, the Saxon of the South makes a similar demand. He will possess this region of promise, he says, and take with him his subject race, his serfs and vassals, to work it, not for themselves, but for him; and to give plausibility to his claim, he calls them, not citizens, not people, not even men, but property. Why may not he, as well as the northern man, go to the new territories with his property? To this the northern Saxon replies, that these negroes are not property, but men, and bring with them human influences, not of the highest order; but, whether property or not, they will occupy the land and consume its produce, both and all of which he wants for his own race. Let the southern Saxon go, therefore, to the territories.

if he will, but leave his negroes behind him; or let him take them to regions where the white man cannot work,—to climates congenial to the negro.

The claim of the southern man meets another obstacle in the North. The Saxon is a lover of justice, of humanity, above all, of freedom. He loves these in the abstract; he loves them, too, as the foundation of wealth, and order, and improvement; but he loves them and their results for himself, for his own race. He therefore hates slavery, unless he is the master, and he is not by choice a master. He prefers that all classes where he dwells shall enjoy liberty, equal rights, the means and opportunities of civilization and progress. In the South he is a master, and there he maintains and defends slavery, only because the negro is in the South. In the North there is no race which he is willing to enslave, and therefore his love of liberty and its blessings, acting without check, he is averse to slavery. As the citizen of a northern State, he has banished slavery, and made the negro free, because he cannot be a competitor or an enemy; because slavery, as a legal institution, is not necessary. The land and its fruits, and industry and its rewards, are in the hands of the superior race.

But the Saxon is not merely a northern man, he is a citizen of the United States. In that capacity he is a slaveholder and a master. In that capacity he shares in the wealth that slavery produces, and true to his love of power and of wealth, he is willing enough thus to be a master; he is willing that his race in the South shall hold the negro in bondage. He would do the same thing now in the North, as he once did, were the negro race a large and firmly established part of the population. But the Saxon can work in the north, and he wants all the land and all the work for himself. Therefore he has driven the negro from his borders, not indeed by force, but by opinion; by the pressure of energetic competition—a struggle in which the negro is too weak to engage. This the Saxon will do wherever he can find work for his hands and land to till, in a climate that permits him to work. The silent, irresistible operation of this principle, almost complete in the free states, is going on also throughout the northern slave States, where the negro is disappearing, not so rapidly as the Indian, but steadily and surely, before the conquering industry of the white race. The same spirit is indicated by laws passed from time to time in northern States, prohibiting the residence of the negro within their limits. He is not made a slave in the North for obvious reasons before intimated. The negro population is so small, that no extraordinary precautions are necessary to render it safe. Neither

is slavery necessary to keep it in that place of
social inferiority, which the pride of the superior
race requires. Circumstances and natural laws do
this, without the aid of the legislature. Moreover,
the vast majority of the whites are themselves laboring men; they cannot therefore own slaves.
Ruling as they do the law-making power, they
would not permit the rich to own slaves—for this
toiling and governing class, will endure no competition in its industry by the negro. Neither do the
rich desire to have him for a slave, because the
free, intelligent industry of their own race is far
more productive and profitable, and brings with it
to the employer, no responsibility, no duties, and
no danger.

But though the negro in the North is not a slave,
he is made an outcast and a pariah. There is no
place for him in northern society, no aspirations or
hopes to stimulate him, none of the prizes of life,
wealth, power, respectability, are held out to him,
to nerve his efforts and elevate his desires. He is
governed and protected in all his rights, wholly by
the white race, without his participation. He is
excluded from office, from the hustings, from the
court-house, from the exchange, from every intellectual calling or pursuit, not by legal enactment,
but by his own incapacity, and by opinion; by the
feeling of caste and race, that is to say, by divine

laws, which are stronger than any the legislature can make. He has no civil or political power whatever, by which to protect himself, and he may not lay a finger on one of those three wonderful boxes, the ballot box, the jury box and the cartridge box, which contain the instruments and weapons by which freemen defend their rights. They are for the white race only. A negro governor, legislator, judge, magistrate or juryman does not exist, could not by possibility exist, in the whole North; this race is not only excluded from all political and civil place and power, but the avenues to social rank and respectability are closed against him; or rather they are too steep and difficult for him to climb. He is not a land owner, a manufacturer, a merchant. There is no legal obstacle; but land, machinery and ships are things he cannot manage. There are no black attorneys-at-law, physicians, authors or capitalists in the North. The law opens to the negro these spheres of activity, as widely as to the white man, but they are far beyond the negro's wildest dreams, because beyond his talents. He is thus pushed down by a superior moral and intellectual force, which he can neither comprehend nor resist, into those pursuits which the Saxon, and even the Celt, avoids if he can,—into labors which require the least strength of mind or body, which yield the least profit, and are menial and degrading. The spirit of caste drives the negro out of churches, theatres, hotels, rail-cars, steamboats, or assigns to him, in them, a place apart. It drives him into the cellars, dens, and alleys of towns, into hovels in the country ; and it does all this without laws, without concert or design, without unkindness or cruelty, but unconsciously, simply because it cannot help doing it, obeying thus instinctive impulse, and the immutable, eternal laws by which the races of men are kept apart, and are preserved through countless ages without change. These laws are divine. They execute themselves in spite of party combinations or fanatical legislatures, or philanthropic enthusiasts, or visionary dreamers about human perfectability and the rights of man. These laws have destined the Saxon to command, the negro to obey, and we see, therefore, that without law or by law, the Saxon is the master and the negro the servant, both in the North and in the South.

Such is the state of facts and opinion produced by the natural laws of race, on this fearful subject of slavery. These opinions and facts, being translated into the language of parties and politicians, mean simply, what every newspaper tells us, that the South claims an equal right with the North to possess the territories, which are the common property of both ; that the North claims the right to exclude slavery, in other words, the negro race, from those territories, but at the same time declares that it will respect and maintain slavery in the States where it already exists, so long as they choose to keep it.

These are the opinions of the great majority of the people, to whatever party they may belong. It is impossible for them to have any other opinions. There are in the North some abolitionists, carried away by the enthusiasm of a dominating idea, who dream of emancipation; and there are also some slavery propagandists, who have not yet escaped the influence of party passion and discipline, but every indication of popular feeling, shows that the great masses of the North will obey the instincts of their race, maintain its supremacy and dominion over the negro, and keep liberty and land, and wealth and power for themselves, exclusively, whether in the North or the South.

If such be the sentiment of the northern people, that sentiment must rule the government. It will control the movements of parties, defeat the schemes of politicians, and break through all factitious combinations which seek to restrain it. We have seen the power of this controlling spirit of race showed itself when the issue was joined between North and South, as to which should possess the territory of

Kansas; how, by instant and passionate creation, the Republican party arose; how the northern Democracy immediately abandoned the South. When the North is united on any question, it must govern the country. All elements of strength and command are in the North, because the North is inhabited exclusively by the superior race. Hence its more rapid progress in population, wealth, and the arts of civilization. These have never flourished in Africa, and the South is partly African. The seeds of improvement cannot there strike deep roots and grow to healthy, fruitful plants, as they do in the North, because the sub-soil of society is barren.

Refinement, luxury, culture there may be in the South, among the few, but these do not constitute civilization. They are some only of its flowers and fruits, and even they, can have but a feeble and evanescent growth and life, unless sustained and enriched by the intelligence, morality, energy, aspirations, diversified occupation and exciting emulation of a superior race, filling all the avenues of industry and enterprise. The negro is unequal to such labors, struggles or hopes, and a civilization founded on him, must be sickly and ephemeral. So we are taught by history, so by ethnology, and the comparative statistics of the North and the South of our country, tell the same story, and in

3

most emphatic language. The North, therefore, must govern on all questions that arise between North and South, for the decree of nature herself

"Grants unto dwellers with the pine,
Dominion o'er the palm and vine."

We have seen how the opinions of the North, in relation to slavery, are the result of the laws of race. Are these opinions just and wise, and what is the policy which the North should endeavor to carry out? Perhaps the same laws of race can afford warnings and lessons to guide us.

The contest between the white and the dark, the superior and inferior races of mankind, is not peculiar to this age or to our country. It fills the pages of history, and is going on at this moment all over the world; in India, China, Syria, Turkey, Africa, and America, North and South. The white brings his force of intellect and will, his knowledge and arts. The dark man has on his side his numbers, the climate, and the wealth he produces; wealth to allure, the climate to enervate or destroy; numbers which can neither be civilized nor permanently conquered, but which can corrupt the blood and debase the morals of the higher race. With these he maintains his ground. Saxon nor Celt can colonize the tropics. The English have not done it in India or Africa, nor the French in Algiers. The law of nature, which assigns certain races to appropriate zones of climate, protects and executes itself.

The types of races, at least in their primary classification, are permanent. They never change, and different species do not mingle, so as to constitute a new race; although those nearly allied, as the varieties of the white, may form a people partly of mixed blood, yet the tendency is to separation, as may be seen now in the nations of Europe. The division between white and black is more strictly maintained. The mixed breeds are weak in constitution and unfruitful with each other, and return more speedily to whichever parent stock is favored by the climate and numbers. In our southern States, that is to say, in the cotton states, or extreme South, the negro has found a congenial climate, and obtained a permanent foothold. He can multiply, without fresh blood from his native regions. He can *work* in the South, but the white man cannot. He cannot, like the negro, live and grow there; and would degenerate, and ere long disappear by natural causes, unless his numbers were kept up by emigration from the North, to which he belongs. All influences favor the increase and ultimate ascendency of the black race in our extreme South and the countries around the Gulf of Mexico. The slave trade favors it; the demand for cotton, tobacco, rice, sugar, and other Southern produce, favors it, by encouraging the growth of negro population. The negro multiplies, the white man dwindles and decays. If not a planter, he becomes "poor white trash." Even now, slavery can be maintained where it exists, only by foreign power in alliance with the resident white race, which, as the causes above mentioned continue to operate with greater force, will become more and more dependent on such support. In a society so constituted, there can be virtually two classes only, masters and slaves, the latter a constant source of dread, either in peace or war, unimprovable and essentially barbarous. There can be no educated, wealthy middle class, no skilled mechanics, no intelligent, trustworthy laborers, no "bone and sinew," and sooner or later, from causes external or internal, the negroes will revolt and take possession of the country. Were slavery abolished, the same result would be brought about, more gradually and peaceably. The land would not pay. It would be abandoned by the rich and enterprising, and Africa with barbarism would speedily become supreme. In either case, this seems to be the probable fate of those regions, which events may hasten or retard. Nothing but cotton keeps the white race in our Southern States now. They are not a desirable residence. The climate is unhealthy, and the

conveniences and pleasures of civilization are wanting. The rich lead a nomadic life, spending most
of the year in Europe or the North. They, as well
as those who are obliged to remain, are bound to
the country only by cotton. Meanwhile the cotton land is becoming exhausted. Worn-out plantations multiply. Even at present prices, cotton
can be made profitable only on new, or the small
area of permanently fertile soils. Should the price
ever fall much below the present, by reason of supplies from other regions, a result by no means improbable, then the South would be abandoned to
the negro. Should the spirit of revolt ever be so
diffused among the slaves as to destroy the feeling
of security, also not improbable, the same effect
would be produced. Confidence in the safety of
life and property, is essential to society. All facts,
all tendencies, all causes, therefore, point in one
direction,—the ultimate ascendency of the black
race, in that portion of the country favorable to its
nature.

Neither is this effect so far in the future, as to be
beyond the scope of our politics. The negro increases in the South with tropical luxuriance. His
growth is stimulated by the value of his labor and
by importations of fresh blood from its native
source. We have now four millions, a formidable
number, which settles the question as to the per-

3*

manent establishment of the race in our country.
But the child is now born that will see thirty-six
millions in the Southern States, more by four millions than our present entire population. Thirty-
six millions in seventy-eight years, with perhaps
Hayti, Cuba, Jamaica, and other islands in the
West Indies, by that time in the hands of the
same race. Can this mass of barbarism be governed at all, whether in slavery or freedom, by
white men, who would be willing to live in the
midst of it? The mere figures answer the question, and oppress the mind by the terrible future.
But eighty years is too far off for the vision of our
politicians, who look only to the next election; or
of the majority of our people indeed, engrossed as
they are by the interests of the passing hour. Let
us take a shorter period, then. In fifty years we
shall have sixteen millions; or if that be too re-
mote for the grasp of our attorney-at-law statesmanship, let us look only twenty-five years ahead.
Our four millions will then be eight. Is even this
a manageable number? We have trouble enough
now with four. They are constantly bringing us
to the verge of disunion. They absorb the public
mind, and the thoughts and the time of government,
by the dangers they evoke. They have produced
sectional animosity and strife, where peace and
good will should reign. . They have thrown the ad-

ministration of the law throughout the South, into lynch-law committees, and have forbidden any Northern man to go there, unless he leaves his independence, and freedom of thought and speech behind him. They have destroyed all industry but their own, and made the South dependent upon foreign supplies, for every article which human ingenuity has invented for the comfort and accommodation of man. They must be sentinelled and watched, to protect society from horrors worse than war. They inspire terror during peace, and in case of invasion, would be more fearful than the enemy. By means of their weakness they control our politics; they conquer us by abject submission; they overwhelm us by mere prolific growth; they have manacled our hands and feet with fetters of gold, and, nominally slaves, they are really the masters of our destiny. Our four millions have done all this. What then may we expect of them, when they are eight, sixteen, thirty-six millions? Will they not say, or rather, will not the eternal laws of nature say through them, this land of rice and cotton, of swamps and malaria, is ours, because we alone can live and work in it. It belongs to us by right divine. It is our Africa of the New World, in it we will rule and revel?

Meanwhile, however, alongside of this new Africa, separated only by indistinct and shifting boundaries, its close neighbor, forever, is a new Europe, a vast region, where the white man can live and work, and which he is filling up with the rapidly increasing millions of his race ; a race born to rule, born for liberty, voluntary labor, intellectual progress, the arts, religion and civilization—the only historic race. New Africa is united to this new Europe by political ties, and by other stronger ties which bind together the, as yet, dominant races of each. The two together form a nation, a people, with common interests and hopes, and so far as they can achieve it, a common destiny. Now what is the plain duty of this nation of white men, governing by right of intellectual superiority, the black race established among them; what is its duty as a nation, as a united people, to themselves and to the negro ? If there be any truth in ethnical science, any warning in the lessons of history, a more serious question never was presented for the consideration of a government, whether we regard the present, or the rapidly approaching future.

The negro race, in mind and character, is weak and imperfectly developed, belongs to a lower order of man. Slavery has no other justification, excuse or apology, than this. If this be not true, American slavery is a monstrous wickedness, against which every christian should preach a crusade till, at whatever cost or sacrifice, it be banished from the land. Is it not, then, the obvious duty of the nation which holds the negro in subjection, to prevent the growth of a race which is incapable of liberty or civilization, which is just so much heathenism and barbarism wherever it exists; of a population which forms no part of the people, which is alien and hostile, and thus a source, not of strength but of weakness; of a race which can be enslaved, which must be held in subjection by some system equivalent to slavery, and which, from natural causes, increases so rapidly, as to threaten, at no distant day, to escape all control, and to banish, exterminate, or bring down to its own level, where it is planted and luxuriates, the superior race by which it is now governed? Surely no argument is necessary to prove that a nation must be happier, wiser, richer, more powerful and more glorious, where the whole people are of the strongest, most intellectual and most moral race of mankind, than where any portion of the people are degraded by nature, and incapable of progress or civilization. Barbarism is barbarism, whether in Africa or America; and a country inhabited by barbarians cannot be civilized. Just in proportion to the number of its barbarians, is it wanting in the elements of civilization, and just in that proportion, too, is it weak and liable to overthrow, from dangers within and without. The history of the world, from the dim annals of the most distant past, to the journalism of the present hour, proves this. What destroyed the civilization of ancient India, Egypt, and Persia, but the gradual predominance of the dark races of the South, favored by climate, over the white race of the North, which founded that civilization and maintained it, so long as the race could maintain its ascendency.

To the same cause, the admixture and degradation of blood, has been attributed with every semblance of reason, the decay of Grecian and Roman power, art, literature and philosophy; all of which sprang from the intellect of the northern race, and declined as that race melted away before the dark races of the South, aided by a climate suited to their nature.* What does modern Europe show, but the energetic conflict of the superior races with each other, growing stronger from conflict, and evolving letters, arts, liberty, government, wealth and history, from their heroic struggles and labors, as the golden harvest rises out of the ploughed and harrowed soil, wherever those races fill the country, as they do in France, England, Germany and all the north. During the same period, the south of Europe, Italy, Spain, Turkey and Greece, has been growing weaker and weaker, until, at length, all these na-

* Gobineau, sur l'inegalité des Races humaine, vol. 2.

tions are in reality governed by the stronger races, represented by what are called the "Great Powers," and are maintained by them in nominal, sickly, feeble, fictitious nationalities and independence, only because those Great Powers are jealous of each other. If we look to the East, the picture is still more sombre, because the predominant race is darker. Over India, Persia, Syria, Egypt, the seats of antique civilization, the fountain-sources of modern philosophy, poetry and religion, has settled the thick shades of ignorance and barbarism. Liberty, literature, art and government, have died out, because the only race whose mind spontaneously produces these fruits, has died out. The movements of their people, whether in peace or war, are unknown; they are not worth recording, and there is no one to record them. Like the fights of the wild beasts of the jungle, or the migrations of birds or buffaloes; like the quarrels of savage tribes in Africa or North America, governed not by ideas but by animal needs or instincts, what these races of human animals do, forms no part of history. They can give us no knowledge or wisdom, and their actions and habits are interesting only as scientific facts, to the physiologist, to the ethnologist, to the student of that mysterious creature, man, who presents such varied aspects in his manifold nature. If we look to our side of the Atlantic, the same story is told by the West Indies, and Central and South America, all of them colonized by the white race, which, in all, has proved too weak for the climate, the aboriginal Indian and the negro, and is receding before them. The mongrel population, arising from these, cannot maintain free government, can scarcely keep up a waning and feeble civilization, and makes no progress in industry, wealth, letters or the arts. It is rapidly going back to the original type of the country, or to the negro, who finds there a congenial home.

These are the teachings of history, and also of the passing hour. Shall we heed them and endeavor to check the extension of Africa in our country, with its barbarism and its weakness, with the moral blight and manifold curses of slavery that accompany it, or shall we give it scope and encouragement to grow and spread, wherever reckless cupidity may choose to take it? Shall we keep our broad stretches of fertile land for the Saxon, that he may found thereon an empire of liberty, christianity and intellectual culture, to endure and flourish for ages, or shall we plant them with the negro race, and devote them to ignorance, slavery, fetichism and barbarism? This is the question which events have at length put fairly and squarely to us. We, the white race, who own this country, who are the natural masters of the negro, who have, therefore, the right and the power to decide the question, are now called on to decide it, in our national, corporate character, as a people and a government. Can any one doubt how we shall decide it? To doubt is to deny our history since the dawn of civilization, to deny all the marking qualities of our race. We will decide it if we can, as a united people; but if we cannot, if cotton and slavery and the negro, have already weakened our Southern brethren by their spells and enchantments, so that the South cannot decide according to the traditions and impulses of our race, then we of the North, will still decide it, as by right we may,—by right of reason, of race, and of law.

The policy, therefore, of restraining the growth of the negro race within those limits of climate, where he alone can work and thrive, is indicated by the qualities of that race, and accords also with the dominant characteristics of the white. These characteristics have from the beginning, ruled the conduct of government, which has uniformly permitted or excluded the negro under the name of slavery, according to the conditions of climate. Wherever the Saxon could work, he has claimed the soil for himself alone. Wherever he could not work, he has, either in his individual or national character of slaveholder, taken or allowed the negro to be taken, to work for him. Natural laws would have

brought about this result without the aid of the
legislature, for these laws confine each race to its
appropriate portion of the earth. The climate in
which the negro can work and thrive repels the
white, whilst the negro is excluded from the North,
both by the climate and by the competition of the
more intellectual and energetic race. If all the
laws of the Northern States prohibiting slavery
were at once repealed, this state of things would
remain unaltered. The negro is not only disappearing from those States where he is free, but also
from those where slavery is still permitted, and
where the climate allows the white man to obtain
a footing as a laborer. The question, which race
shall possess the national territories, has for another
reason ceased to be of practical importance, and
cannot much longer be kept alive, even as a theme
for party agitation. There are no territories now
belonging to the government, from which the white
race is excluded by the climate; there are none
therefore in which the negro can be planted and
grow. Neither laws nor party conventions, nor
Supreme Court decrees can put him, or keep him
there, against the higher law of nature.

There are, however, two other modes by which
the growth and extension of the negro may be
stimulated, that present more serious difficulties.

One is the acquisition of new land in a climate suited to his nature; the other is fresh importations from Africa. The indications are plain enough, that this terrible and protean slavery question will soon assume these shapes, and present these two issues to the nation;—further annexation of tropical territory, and the revival of the slave trade. The one is a necessary consequence of the other, for the land is worthless without negroes to till it, they alone being able to till it. The negroes we now have are all needed for the land we now possess, as their price proves. If we get more land therefore, we must have more negroes, just as a farmer, when he buys more acres, must increase his force.

Unfortunately, these two projects appeal directly to the ruling passions and marking traits of the Saxon;—his love of conquest and adventure, his love of colonizing and founding, his love of material prosperity and profitable industry, his love of supremacy and control. These qualities have sent him all over the world in quest of land to subdue and cultivate and possess, and have encircled the earth with his drumbeat and his canvas, his language, his laws, and his arts. Tempting, indeed, are the fertile regions in and around the Gulf of Mexico, rich in the productions for which the markets of the world open their hungry mouths, and occupied now by a weak, effete, mongrel, withered race, who

cannot govern them, or cultivate them, or bring out
of their soil a tithe of its wealth, or defend them
against an invader. They invite us by their allur-
ing looks, by their syren smiles, by their bewitch-
ing beauty, and say to our valor, our enterprise,
our daring, mounting ambition;—come and take us
and our delights; we belong not to the weak, but
to the strong and bold. 'Tis the old story; the
Cleopatra of the South, the " serpent of the Nile,"
entangling the sensual, brave, athletic and conquering northern Anthony, in her silken meshes of dalli-
ance, lapping him in luxury and sloth, kissing away
his manhood, courage, glory, power, and " provinces."

> " The barge she sat in, like a burnished throne,
> Burned on the water; the poop was beaten gold,
> Purple the sails, and so perfumed, that
> The winds were love-sick with them; the oars were silver,
> Which to the tune of flutes kept stroke, and made
> The water which they beat to follow faster,
> As amorous of their strokes."

So sits the queen of the Antilles, and her charm-
ing sisters in their ambrosial summer sea. From
them all,

> " A strange, invisible perfume hits the sense,"

from them and the adjacent shores, redolent of

orange groves, of sugar and cotton and tobacco,
promising land, ease, wealth, and power, to enterprise and courage, whilst Africa offers her dusky
millions of docile laborers, feebly and inefficiently
protected now, by repealable laws.

Indications are not wanting, to show the force of
this temptation. Reiterated and exaggerated com-
plaints of injuries and insults offered to us by the
weak and decaying governments who possess this
El Dorado, are ostentatiously paraded in presidential
messages, as pretexts for invasion. Fillibustering
expeditions for the same purpose, are connived at
by our government, and eagerly supported by
Southern opinion. Northern capital sends slave-
ships to Africa, and cargoes of captured negroes
are landed on our southern shores, without punishment, and with scarcely the mockery of trial. The
natural laws of trade, by which demand creates
supply, favor this influence of the characteristics
of our people. All these causes and tendencies
prove, that the tropics are the natural home of
the dark race, to which it is led by irresistible laws,
and which it is destined to fill and occupy. Afri-
cans and Chinese are brought now by annually
increasing thousands to the West Indies. St. Do-
mingo is already under the dominion of the negro,
and but for the European governments which own
them, Cuba, and the other islands of the same

4*

group, would speedily fall under his power, as they are now almost exclusively occupied by his race. In Brazil, Mexico, Venezuela, and Central America, the Spanish blood of the conquerors is rapidly running out, and the mixed breeds are resolving themselves into the native Indian or the negro. The white race cannot colonize these regions, cannot build up in them an enduring, Christian, European civilization. It can hold them only as provinces, governing their inhabitants as a subject people, by military power, as England holds and governs India, and France Algiers.

Now what is our duty and our policy as a nation,—as a government? What is the duty of the Northern States, who can, if they choose, control the government, as to these inseparably connected questions—the annexation of tropical territory, and the revival of the slave trade? Shall we yield to the allurements of this garden of Armida, and send thither our own race, to have its blood corrupted by amalgamation, and its energies weakened by the climate, finally to be exterminated by the negro, or sink to his level? Shall we permit our love of power and of gain to become rapacity and cruelty? Shall we degrade our souls and blemish our name, by wars of conquest on lying pretexts against weak neighbors, or by hunting negroes in Africa, trafficking with savage slave-captors and stirring up strife between barbarous tribes, to obtain supplies for our markets? Such things have been done ere now in the world, and by Saxons; nay, are doing at this moment. They accord but too well with the domineering, encroaching, grasping spirit of the race; and the temper of our people, their passionate love of money and of territory, justifies alarm. At present, there is strife between the North and the South; but it has been caused chiefly, almost wholly, by the bold attempt to plant the negro where the Saxon alone should dwell, and by the acts of violence and aggression which accompanied that attempt. When the quarrel on this subject ceases, as it soon will, should the South point to Cuba, Mexico, and Central America, and speak of cotton, sugar, tobacco, and coffee; of acquisition, expansion, wealth, and dominion to the northern man, the song will be a music to which Saxon ears always have listened, and always will listen, with delight. The eloquence of the South can veil even the repulsive features of the slave-trade. Slavery, we may be told, nay, we are told, is a blessing to the negro. It educates, christianizes, elevates him. The horrors of the middle passage are caused by the law. Legalize the traffic, and the slave-ship will become as comfortable as any other. Why not, then, permit African as well as Irish emigration? Dressed in this garb, the slave-trade may offer, especially to the eyes of self-interest, willing to be convinced, the aspect of a Christian mission, to rescue Africa from barbarism and idolatry.

Such are the dangers to which the tendencies of race are leading us. We should resist them while we may. The revival of the slave-trade would, by the infusion of fresh barbarism, lower the character of our negro population, multiply its numbers, which already increase too rapidly, add to the perils of servile war, and degrade our moral sentiment and self-respect, by a loathsome traffic, condemned by the enlightened humanity of the civilized world. It would also hasten the period of African domination in the South.

We can get the coveted territories only by war; war not merely with the people who possess them, but probably also with European nations, already jealous of our increasing power. When got, they would invite aggression, present vulnerable points, and could be held only by a large military force. A standing army, therefore, and foreign wars, would be the results of such an acquisition.

The people of these territories, though weak and inferior to ourselves, are nevertheless within the pale of civilized, Christian nations. They are, therefore, under the protection of the law of nations. Without a gross violation of that law, we could not, by whatever process they might be an-

nexed, disregard the rights of these people. We
could not govern them as a subject race,—as England
governs India,—as we govern our negroes. These
people would participate, therefore, in our liberty,
our constitution, and our laws. These mongrel, decaying, ignorant, morally and intellectually inferior
races, would thus become our fellow-citizens, would
share in the government of our country, and influence or control, by their votes, the interests, the
will, and the destiny of the North—of the Saxon.
The laws of race prohibit such a partnership. It
would break the Union. The Saxon would not live
with Mexicans, Indians, half-breeds, and worn-out
Spaniards, on terms of equality, or share their destiny, or permit them to partake in his authority
over his own country. According to our constitution,
acquired territories must become States. Whether
political power were granted to the original inhabitants or withheld, and the supremacy given to the
conquering race, the contest between South and
North would be revived with tenfold bitterness.
Conflicting interests and claims would again create
a struggle for power, and the result would be, separation, and a Southern confederacy, or, more probably, another failure added to the list of abortive
Southern Republics. The warnings and lessons
offered, therefore, by the laws of race, plainly indi-
cate, that neither by the acquisition of new terri-

tory, nor by the revival of the slave-trade, would it be wise to encourage the growth of the negro under our government, nor to increase his influence over our fate.

Another question of great importance is, how shall we govern the negro? That we must govern him is plain, as already stated, because of his attributes and of ours. Accordingly we do govern him, wholly without his consent or participation, both in the North and the South. But in the South we make him a slave. Is this wise, is it morally right? In the North, he is refused political liberty or power over public affairs, and the reason is, that he is unfit—permanently and naturally unfit—to exercise that power. In the South, he is deprived of personal liberty, or power over himself. This is a great wrong, unless it be true that he is unable to exercise this power also, for his own good and the good of society. On the inherent, unalterable qualities of the negro, hinges the whole question of slavery. Fortunately for our justification, unfortunately for our country, all the researches of science, all the annals of the past, and all the facts of the present hour, prove that the negro is fit for servitude, that he requires guidance and protection, naturally seeks them, and renders in return, labor and obedience. Servitude arises from the relation of strength to weakness; and the negro is adapted to it, by his want of intellectual power, his feebleness of will, his docility, his good nature. He is submissive, and neither hates nor inspires hatred. He is improvident, and incapable of forethought, because in Africa, forethought was unnecessary to supply his wants. He is indolent for the same reason, but acquires habits of industry under the control of a superior will. In his native regions, his freedom was the freedom of savage life. He did not leave his nature behind him when he came here, and if released from the sustaining and directing power of the white race, he would return again to savage life. It is remarkable, moreover, that slavery exists in Africa. The black races of that country differ in mental and physical qualities and force. The stronger enslave the weaker, and those races that are slaves there, are those which have been brought here. The internal evidence of the negro's nature, showing him to be fit for slavery, is corroborated by the fact, that he has been, in all ages, contented and submissive in slavery. This is true of no other race. The Mongol, the North American Indian, cannot be enslaved; they would resist. The aborigines, of South America and the West Indies, withered and perished under slavery. It suits only the negro, who lives and labors, thrives and increases, under its protecting care.

Slavery is servitude established by law; servitude during life, for one who cannot aspire to a higher lot; servitude of a race, fitted by nature for that lot. It provides for the negro the guidance and support through life that he needs, and expresses the relation which his nature bears to that of the white man. Slavery, moreover, performs the duty of magistrates, police, prisons, poor-houses and hospitals, for the negro race in the South, without expense to government, and far more efficiently than any government could perform them. Slavery is not in itself a good thing; on the contrary, it is an evil thing, and bears fruit according to its nature. But we have the negro, and therefore we must have slavery. Our system of slavery, doubtless, is far from perfect. Its chief defects arise from the predominance given to the mercenary element of the relation over the benevolent, in the laws of the Southern States. These laws declare, that a slave is a mere chattel, and the Supreme Court of the United States has declared so too.

But the laws of nature say, servitude is the natural relation between the negro and the white race; that a slave is a man, and not a thing, and, therefore, entitled to justice and humanity; that he has rights which impose duties on the master, and that the dominant race, having power over the negro, is responsible for his well-being. The laws of the South, and the decision in the case of Dred Scott, contradict these truths; but they are affirmed by the general sentiment and practice of the Southern people, and by the Constitution, which correctly describes a slave as a "*person* held to service or labor," using this language emphatically, as is well known, for the express purpose of denying that slaves are property; a doctrine worthy only of slave-traders and African tribes, from whom it was derived.

Servitude is the natural position of the negro, and slavery places him in that position. It is the system which the Southern Saxon has adopted for governing the large and increasing numbers of the black race with which he lives,—which he must govern for his own safety and prosperity. With all its defects, evils and dangers, it does, in fact, accomplish its object. Southern society is protected from either the violence, or the pauperism, or vice, of the negro race, whilst that race is also protected by slavery, and maintained in a condition superior to that of its brethren in the North, or in Africa. The negro is worth our care, not only because of his own good qualities, but because he has power over us, which we cannot get rid of. Under all possible circumstances, and for all future time, the negro will be our companion, and form part of our population. Upon him depend the wealth and pros-

5

perity of the South, for what would become of these without cotton? The manufactures and commerce of Europe and of the North, are sustained also by cotton and other Southern produce, the result, either exclusively or chiefly, of negro labor.

The question, therefore, of how to govern the negro, is of interest to us and to the world. If it be true, that slavery or servitude established and regulated by law, accords with his nature and with ours,—is a benefit to him and to us,—then slavery harmonizes with those obligations of morality which neither men nor nations may disobey with impunity, and it is our duty, as a nation, to maintain slavery, and, if possible, ameliorate and improve it. It is the duty also of the North, to the men of their own race in the South, heartily and cordially to support and assist them, in their difficult task of governing a subject race, whose increasing numbers threaten, at no distant day, to break down all barriers of restraint. They, the men of the South, have this task imposed on them, and are engaged in fronting its dangers, enduring its evils, and are responsible for its results. They, therefore, should have control over slavery, to keep it, to alter and amend it, or to abolish it, as they think fit.

It has been shown before, that the public opinion of the northern people, on the subject of slavery, arises, necessarily, from the respective characteristies of the negro and the Saxon races. The same characteristics or organic laws, dictate a line of policy in harmony with that sentiment, and show that our government ought to prevent the extension of the negro into any territories now possessed by the nation, which afford a home and sphere of useful labor to the white race; that the growth of the negro should not be encouraged, either by the acquisition of new territory, or by importations from Africa, and that the supremacy of the superior race, in the Southern States, should be supported, by maintaining slavery in those States, so far as the action of the general government is necessary for that object.

It is satisfactory to find that the principles thus disclosed by the philosophy of race, are also in the Constitution. The reason is, that it necessarily grew out of and was controlled by those principles. By the powers it grants and the duties it imposes, the government has authority to rule and regulate the national territories, to make war and treaties, to prohibit the slave-trade, to suppress domestic insurrection, and to cause fugitives from " service or labor" to be returned to those " to whom such service or labor may be due." These provisions cover the whole ground, as if inspired by prophetic wisdom. They are sufficient for the security of the South, and for all the wise and just plans or purposes of the North. Let us abide by the Constitution, and so deal with the negro and with slavery, as to reap what of good they produce, diminish their evils and dangers, and postpone, as far as we can, the dark day of disunion and Southern decline, if that day be indeed approaching.

MR. DALLAS AND LORD BROUGHAM.*

"Are these things necessities?
Then let us meet them like necessities."
HENRY IV., PART II.

SOME weeks ago, there was a meeting in London of the International Statistical Congress. Prince Albert presided, and the American Minister was present. One of the members of this scientific assembly, also present, was a colored man from Canada; and in the course of the proceedings, Lord Brougham publicly called the attention of Mr. Dallas to that fact. Mr. Dallas made no reply. His experience enabled him, no doubt, to judge correctly of the proprieties of his place and the occasion, and it is only just to him to believe, that he had sufficient reasons for remaining silent; that he did what, under the circumstances, was right to do.

---

* This Essay was written for the North American and United States Gazette, and published in that journal, August 18, 1860. The author re-prints the article here, because the topics discussed in it are pertinent to the argument of the foregoing Essay.

5*

Had there been no such reasons, however, the objects of the Society, the character of the assembly, the presence of the dusky member from Canada, and the speech of Lord Brougham, all afforded a scene, an audience and an opportunity for telling some truths about slavery, worth telling to the English people. Let us suppose that no rules of etiquette, no fears of compromising official dignity by exciting what perhaps might have become an unseemly discussion, had interfered, would it not have produced a good effect on the minds of the cultivated persons present, and on the public opinion of England and America, had Mr. Dallas made something like the following

Speech.

MR. CHAIRMAN :—

I am a guest of this learned Society, rather than a participator in its proceedings. I came here to look on and listen, not to speak. The remarks, however, of the noble Lord who has just addressed you, induce me to crave for a few moments the attention of this meeting. His Lordship has called on me to notice the fact, that a man of the African race is here present, received and treated as an associate, by the eminent gentlemen around me. I

will not assume, I will not suppose that Lord
Brougham intended anything offensive to me or to
the country I have the honor to represent, by what
he said. His fame is so widely spread in Europe
and in America, that all the world knows him to
be opposed to slavery. He is opposed to it, I feel
sure, not as an enemy to the United States, but as
a philosopher and statesman, on what he deems
just and reasonable grounds, and he no doubt meant
to say, by his pointed allusion to me,—" Behold,
Mr. Dallas, behold men of America, here in England, the foremost nation of the world, is a negro,
received as a companion and an equal, in a circle,
composed of some of the brightest names of their
country, in social rank, in literature and science !
Why, then, do you make him a slave ?"

I must believe that the person referred to, finding him as I do, in such distinguished society, has
qualities which render him in some degree worthy
of his companions. It very often happens in my
country, that men of his race possess estimable vir-
tues, and are remarkable for truth, honesty, and
fidelity ; it sometimes happens that, under favorable circumstances, they make considerable intellectual progress, and acquire knowledge, which does
not imply mental powers of a high order. But we
have some acquaintance at home with negroes.
There are four millions of them in our Southern

States; and I can assert with confidence, that our experience is like that of all other countries, of all other ages recorded by history, and that examples even of the moderate endowments and attainments I have mentioned, are the exceptions, not the rule. The race is not gifted with the force of character or intellect that fits it to originate or sustain a native, independent civilization. It does not produce artists, poets, and philosophers—not even soldiers, orators, lawyers, and statesmen. There are no negro Shakspeares, Raphaels, or Bacons; no Marlborough or Wellington, no Pitt, Fox, Mansfield, or Brougham, with black skin and woolly hair, either in the past or the present. Even in the humbler spheres of business and industry, the negro is disqualified by nature to conduct the commerce, the manufactures, or the mechanic arts of a civilized community. All these require for their management, mental powers which the negro does not possess. As a general rule, he is fit only for manual labor that requires but little thought; and to achieve in this, valuable results, he must be directed by superior intelligence. He has therefore occupied, wherever he has been associated with the white race, the position of a servile class or caste. He occupies this position in America. In the North as well as in the South, the menial and inferior offices of society are assigned to him, or rather, he falls into them naturally by the operation of laws, which no social or political arrangements, are strong enough to alter or resist.

But in our Southern States we make him a slave. I know that this word has an unpleasant sound to an English ear. There are many in America, also, who do not like it. Nevertheless, slavery exists there, and must exist in some form or other for many years to come, perhaps forever, by reason of the natural laws of race to which I have alluded. We have four millions of negroes in our South, very different, indeed, with few exceptions, from him to whose presence here my attention has been called. They constitute, in fact, a vast mass of ignorance and barbarism, which cannot govern itself, either for their good or ours—which, therefore, we must govern. We, the superior race, have the right, by reason of our superiority, to govern them for our own safety and interest, not neglecting at the same time their well-being. Thus justified, and for the purpose of accomplishing these objects, we have established slavery as a system of government for the negro race, wherever it exists in such numbers as to make slavery necessary; or to speak with more philosophical as well as historical accuracy, slavery has arisen naturally from the contact of the two races. It furnishes, without expense to government, an efficient magistracy and police to main-

tain order and subordination; it enforces industry
and temperance, without poor-houses or prisons; it
promotes the happiness of the negro, by connect-
ing the interest of the master with the health and
strength, the cheerfulness and contentment of the
slave. Slavery, therefore, with us, means care,
guidance, just control, and protection for the negro; it means, also, security, order, enterprise,
wealth, and progress for ourselves. The presence
of the negro race in vast numbers among us, renders slavery a necessity, not a choice. It would
not have been our choice,—for we are quite English in our love of liberty. Being a necessity,
we have used it, not cruelly or oppressively, but
in a manner worthy a people that is proud to
number Alfred and Hampden among its ancestors,
and regards *magna charta* and the common law, as
its richest inheritance. The theoretical harshness
of the system is modified and softened in practice
by the character of those who apply it. The negro
has been confided by Providence to the care and
keeping of the magnanimous Saxon race—of that
race which has built up in this Island such a splendid
edifice of knowledge, liberty, wealth, and power;
which has based its mighty and beneficent civilization on the eternal maxims of truth, justice, and
humanity, and which has erected on the same
secure foundations, an empire in the West, whose

giant proportions are as yet faintly traced by the hand of time. These two great branches of this noble family, I humbly hope, and trust, and believe, are destined to inherit the earth. May they grow and prosper, and be united in friendship as in blood; and may they rule in the East and the West, for the good of the world.

The care of the negro has been thus confided to us in America, as a trust. We have power over him; we are therefore responsible for his welfare. I will not now speak of the perils and difficulties that accompany this trust, or of the evils and calamities it brings with it. We know these well enough at home; and those present may know something of them, too, from many popular works in the current literature of the day. Nor will I deny short-comings in the performance of our duty. Irresponsible power is ever liable to abuse, and mercenary motives are not the best protection for helpless weakness. In proof of this, if proof were needed, I might point to Ireland and India, cases where an inferior race has been subjected to the power of England, of whom England has been and is, the trustee. I refer to them in no invidious spirit, for I believe that all here present will agree with me, that in the government of each of these dependencies, there has been much to deplore, and much to condemn.

So it has been with our treatment of the negroes. Nevertheless we are not ashamed of slavery. We do not apologize for it; we justify it by pointing to its results. Such is the necessary imperfection of all human institutions, that in speaking of a system that operates on large masses of men, we must be satisfied with general effects, though particular cases of hardship are to be regretted, and if possible remedied. Slavery is an out-growth of Africa, which, with Africa, has been transported to our shores. There is nothing excellent or desirable in the nature of either, but the presence of the one has made the other necessary. Without Africa we should not have had slavery, but having both, we must make the best of them; disarm them, so far as we can, of their mischievous tendencies; convert them if we can, into instruments of good. The justification of slavery is in the evils it has prevented, and the benefits it has conferred, not on us alone, but on the world. It has made of the negroes, an orderly and industrious laboring class, well fed, well clothed, on the whole, kindly treated. Of the suffering that is caused by want, by excessive toil, by unrestrained vice, and by punishment inflicted by the law, they endure less than any laboring class in Europe. If deprived of the protection and wholesome restraint afforded by slavery, they would become helpless paupers through indolence and license, and relapse speedily into African barbarism; wretched themselves, and destructive to the social fabric under whose shelter they now live and thrive.

Whilst slavery is thus a benefit to the negro, by providing for his wants and supplying to his labor the intelligent guidance it requires, by means of that labor, vast tracts of fertile land have been cultivated, that would else have remained a wilderness, and made to contribute to the comfort and accommodation of man. I need not enumerate the products of slave-labor, which freight so largely the commerce of all nations, which employ therefore so much capital and industry, and supply so many wants and luxuries. I will mention only cotton, that wonderful plant, which in some of its forms, enters every household, however high, or however humble, in Europe and America. How much of comfort, cleanliness, and refinement has it given to the poor, how much of these, and of elegance, and beauty too, has it furnished to the rich. Cotton is the basis of the wealth and prosperity of our Southern States, and enters largely as an element of the growing power of the North. But an article of such universal use becomes necessarily a part of the foundation of general commerce and of the wealth of nations. If it has enriched us, has it not enriched England too, and in ampler measure?

6

Look at your newspapers, and the daily reports of your markets; at your statistics of commerce and manufactures, and see what a lordly and commanding part, cotton plays in your affairs. It gives to us who grow it, who have the responsibility, the risks and the evils of the system of labor that produces it, an annual income of less than two hundred millions of dollars; it gives to you who manufacture it, who send it abroad in your ships over all the world, a yearly profit of many hundred millions of pounds sterling. Some of the richest towns and counties in England owe their wealth to cotton. It affords food and employment to many thousands of Englishmen who else would want both; it furnishes profit on many millions of English capital; it has helped therefore, in no small degree, to erect the towering structure of English manufactures and commerce. By creating a home market, and a supply of manure, cotton has also largely promoted the growth of English agriculture, and has thus supported the splendor of many a noble home, as well as the comfort of the farm-house and the cottage. This wonderous growth of population, industry, and wealth, thus produced by cotton, must be sustained by it. Take away from beneath the massy fabric, the delicate fibres of this little plant, and I have the authority of your own leading journal for saying, that the power and prosperity of

England, the order of society, and the stability of the throne itself, would be in danger. I say this from no envious or grudging sentiment. You are welcome to our cotton,—nay it is a matter of business,—you pay for it. If you make more out of it than we do, it is a fair reward of your ingenuity, skill and statesmanship. I allude to the subject merely, to remind you that cotton is the result of slave labor; that without slavery, that labor would be inefficient and unproductive; that therefore, the hoes of our slave-gangs on the Mississippi, are building up the edifice of English wealth and power, as the trowel of the stone-mason erects the walls of a palace; that if slavery be an evil, we in America bear all the brunt of it, and receive a part only of the gain; and that if it be a wrong and a crime, England shares with us the guilt, for she does as much to sustain it as we do.

It may be said, moreover, that the origin of slavery belongs to the colonial period of our history. England landed the first negro on our shores, and planted there an institution, which has struck its roots so deeply, and bears such tempting and golden, though also bitter fruits, that it seems to be part of our destiny forever. If slavery be a crime, therefore, England is *particeps criminis*, and it does not lie in her mouth to reproach us with it, more especially as she enjoys its abundant harvest, bearing herself none of the heat and burden of the day. In one of the noblest dramas of your—I mean of our greatest poet, a guilty king tries to pray, but cannot;

> " Forgive me my foul murder !
> That cannot be, since I am still possessed
> Of those effects for which I did the murder,
> My crown, mine own ambition and my Queen.
> May one be pardoned and retain the offence ?"

If we are guilty, so is England, and both to her penitence for her share of the crime, and to her condemnation of our share, the mills of Manchester are an answer.

It would ill become me, however, in such a presence as this, when attempting to justify slavery, to confine my argument to the mere material view of the question, momentous as that really is;—to say that slavery is a source of wealth to us and to the world, that it maintains social peace and order in a large portion of our country, and that it secures also the physical well-being of the subject race. The reply is obvious, that being as we are, the guardians of the negro, we are bound to look to something higher than our own selfish good or his bodily needs, and to provide for his moral and intellectual improvement. At least, we may fairly be required to show, that slavery is no bar to such improvement. It would be a sad thing indeed, if true, that these four million negroes of ours, are well fed and clothed, only that they may toil for our mercenary advantage, and at the same time by our laws and our practice, are intentionally kept in a state of mental and moral degradation. I admit that no temporal good to them or to us, could justify such tyranny. And herein lies the difficulty of the case, felt in America more deeply than anywhere, because to us it seems well-nigh hopeless. But the evil arises from the nature of the negro, and not from slavery. He makes no spontaneous moral or intellectual progress, whether a slave or free; he never has made any in his native regions. He has never risen, at any period of his history, even to the low grade of Chinese civilization. He acquires no arts, he builds no cities or ships, he invents no machinery, he paints no pictures, he writes no books, he forms no organized communities, he makes no laws, he cannot appreciate truth or beauty, and he is a fetich worshipper at all times and all places, if left to himself. He is naturally a savage and a heathen, and may enjoy in Africa such happiness as belongs to that condition. But in that condition he cannot remain, when he forms part of a civilized community; we cannot permit him to remain in it, both for his own sake and for ours. What, then, are we to do? We

6*

cannot raise him, he cannot raise himself to our level; he cannot take care of himself amid the energetic struggles of a superior race. He would sink to lower depths than his original barbarism, and our four millions of his race would become a dangerous and intolerable mass of ignorance, degradation and pauperism. He must, therefore, be governed, guided, cared for; and slavery, which gives him a governor and care-taker, does not depress, but elevates him. It supplies the want of his nature, a directing mind. Without slavery, he would fall into a state far worse for him, that of a slave without a master. In contact or competition with the white race, he would be everybody's slave, and no one would be bound by duty, or induced by interest, to support or protect him. Our slaves in America are not without religious instruction, and the arts of industry which they are taught, and association with the white race, are an education, imperfect indeed, but superior to that of Africa; and without slavery they would get none at all. They have been elevated by this education. The race now with us is superior to its brethren in Africa,—to its ancestors who first landed on our shores. This is well known, and is made manifest whenever the native African is brought to our country, as he sometimes is, in captured slave ships.

I have said that I could not but believe the

" colored gentleman" from Canada, to possess talents and education, which make him a very rare exception to the general character of his race, else he would not be found in such good company. What fortunate circumstances in his history have produced such a result, I do not know. I would not venture to assert that slavery encourages, or even permits such a development of mind as he no doubt exhibits, for I have never seen a negro, whether a slave or free, whom I considered worthy to be a member of this learned society, or the companion of the cultivated and distinguished gentlemen around me. Nevertheless it is true, that negroes do often, as slaves, rise to employments which require thought and skill, and which imply integrity. Many can read and write ; they become mechanics, sometimes book-keepers, and are frequently entrusted with the management of farms and plantations, and with the direction and control of their fellow-laborers. Slavery, therefore, if it depresses, also elevates. It elevates the mass, and works well on the whole. That it is the best possible system, as now constituted and administered, by which to govern the large and increasing numbers of the negro race in America, I will not affirm. Time and experience may improve it. But it is that which we now think the best, though we are not entirely satisfied with it, for it produces evil as well as good. We would gladly exchange it for a better system, did we know of one, but the interests at stake are too important for experiment or rash innovation. We therefore maintain slavery, not because we do not love liberty, but because we believe the negro unfit for it, and because we believe slavery, in some form, or the complete subordination of the black to the white race, in harmony with natural laws, and essential to the social security, and to the wealth, progress and power of our country.

For all these reasons, a system of caste has grown up in the North as well as the South of the United States, similar to that which prevailed for so many centuries in the grand and noble civilization of ancient India, founded on inequality of race; the black having been there, as with us, the servile and lowest. With this system, the exclusiveness of caste has been introduced. It is not the custom in the United States, for white and black to meet on terms of equality, and this arises, not from hatred or contempt of the negro, who is neither hateful nor despicable, but from pride of race. This feeling is by no means inconsistent with mutual respect and affection between individuals of the two races; for such sentiments are very common—more especially between master and slave,—and throw a softening veil over the harsher features of the relation. I confess I am not without this pride or prejudice, if

you will, myself. Though I know it to be the result of education and association, it has the force
of instinct. Nevertheless, I blame not others who
are free from such feelings, more especially those
of another country, who have not been subjected
to the influences which have formed my sentiments
on this subject. I think it moreover prudent and
proper, that a traveller, especially if he represent
his own country, should conform to the customs
and manners of the people he visits. Were I minister to Rome, I would, if such be the usage, kneel
and kiss the slipper of the Pope; if to China, I
would observe all the frivolous ceremonial of its
court etiquette, and try to eat with chop-sticks.
In like manner, being here, minister to England,
and finding a negro moving in the highest circles of
English society, I cheerfully acquiesce, repress any
exhibition of repugnance or surprise, and should
have taken no notice of the circumstance, had not
my attention been publicly called to it, by the distinguished and noble Lord, whose remarks have induced me to trespass thus much on the indulgence
of this meeting.

This is a meagre sketch of what Mr. Dallas might,
and could, and perhaps would have said, had he
deemed it right to say anything. He would have
filled up and enlarged the outline, with illustrations

drawn from the stores of his thought and knowledge, and clothed it with the vesture of his graceful and happy style. It is too bad that England should taunt us with slavery, and all the while grow rich on our cotton, and fat on our corn; the former exclusively the product of slave labor, the latter indirectly so, for cotton produces the English demand for our corn, which makes it grow. Some of our papers are indignant at the speech of Lord Brougham, but this is a mistake, for resentment admits that slavery is a blemish on our national character, that we are insultable on that point, whereas the institution, if not, as some assert a positive blessing, is a necessity, imposed on us by the negro race, and therefore no reproach. The remark of Lord Brougham was no doubt meant for an argument, as he afterwards said it was, not out of place at the meeting of a statistical society, and as such, it should have been answered, if answered at all. If a covert sneer was also intended, that may be lightly borne, if we can refute the argument.

CECIL.

www.ingramcontent.com/pod-product-compliance
Lightning Source LLC
Chambersburg PA
CBHW022022080426
42733CB00007B/684